COMPACT DISC PAGE AND BAND INFORMATION

MMO CD 3707

Music Minus One

RAVEL
The Piano Trio
Cello

TRIO

for Piano, Violin and 'Cello

I.

Maurice Ravel
(1875 - 1937)

Cello

MUSIC MINUS ONE 'CELLO

RAVEL

THE PIANO TRIO

MMO 3707

II.___*Pantoum*

Cello

III.__Passcaille

IV.__Final

MUSIC MINUS ONE 'CELLO

MMO 3707

RAVEL
THE PIANO TRIO

MUSIC MINUS ONE • 50 Executive Boulevard • Elmsford, New York 10523-1325
Tel: (914) 592-1188   Fax: (914) 592-3116
E-mail: mmomus@aol.com   Websites: www.minusone.com *and* www.pocketsongs.com